This book belongs to

_____

_____

_____

_____

INSTRUCTIONS

 It is convenient to clarify that learning how to write by hand in cursive is a medium-term process, therefore it is important that the student stays motivated and does not feel so much pressure to achieve it. Orienting ourselves to this objective, it is suggested not to saturate him with the completion of many worksheets, developing a few worksheets in each session (maximum 4) will produce better results and maintain a good disposition to learn.

 Each worksheet has emoticons in the lower right part, for the parent or guardian to evaluate the student's performance, marking the emoji that represents the achievement obtained:

You can do better, try harder!

You are moving forward, don't give up.

You have done very well. Congratulations!

 Upon completion of all activities, the happy faces will be added up and scored by level, to then obtain the sum of all levels as a final score, which will be considered for the respective awards.

 It is suggested that the father or guardian establish together with the student the awards that will be obtained according to the score obtained at the end of the workbook.

 The format for writing the awards and making the lump sum for all levels is at the end of the book.

LEVEL 1

Basic movements for cursive writing

Here you will learn to:

 Identify the pressure you exert when writing by hand.

 Execute curvilinear, rectilinear, wavy, and basic looping movements to form cursive writing.

Trace the broken lines by applying pressure as indicated by the pattern

Gentle pressure

Normal pressure

Strong pressure

Normal pressure

Draw the lines according to the model.

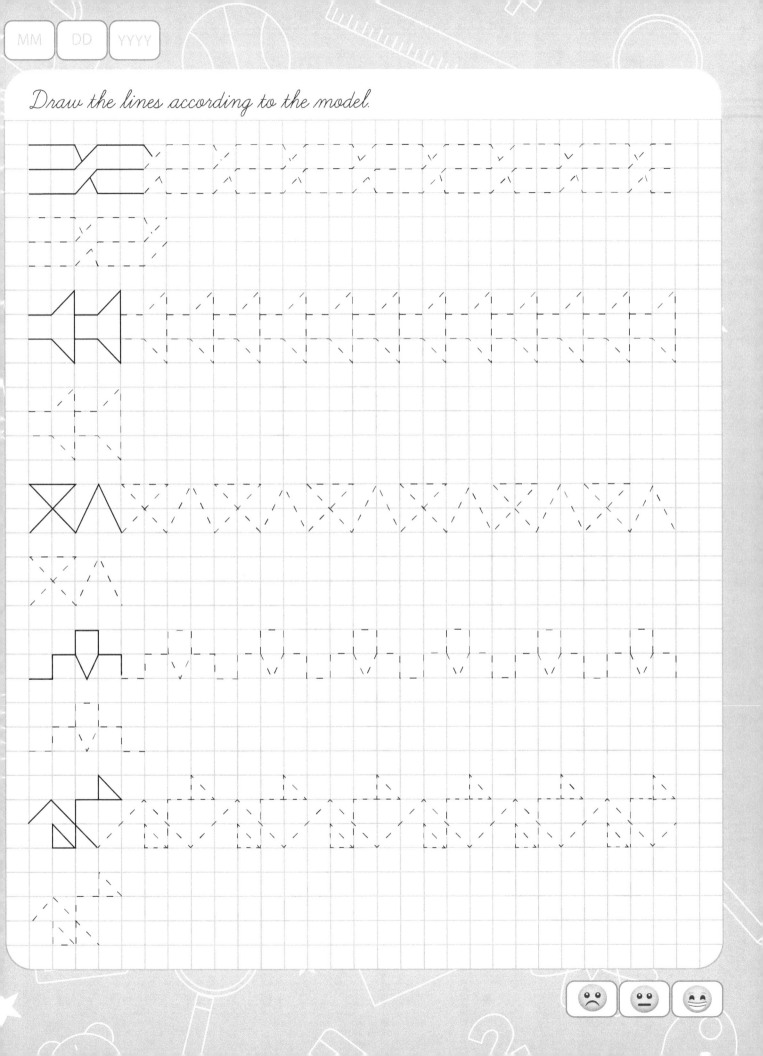

Complete what is missing from each wooden wheel.

Draw the broken lines and color the elements of the solar system to your liking without going out of bounds.

Join the points trying to do it in a straight line.

LEVEL 2

Numbers and visual perception

Here you will learn to:

 Stimulate visual perception as it is very important for the success of cursive writing.

 reproduce the numbers according to the models, find the hidden figure and connect the dots.

Color the hidden drawing in each square.

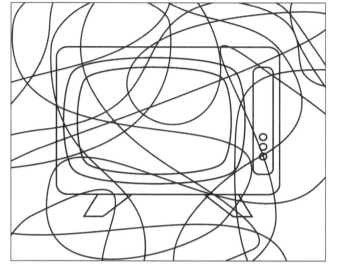
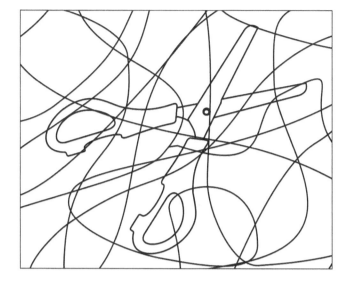
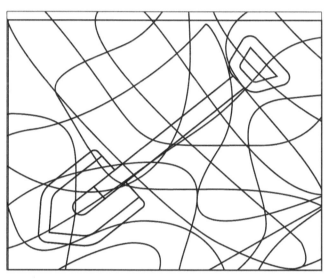

Complete the figure according to the model.

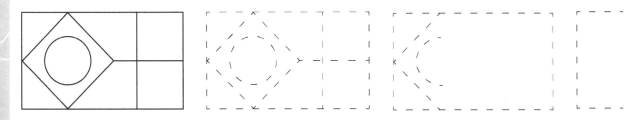

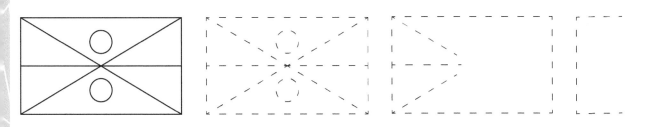

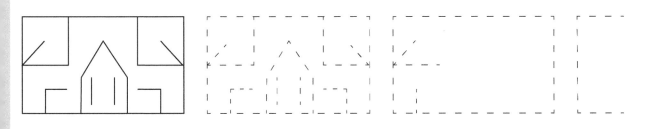

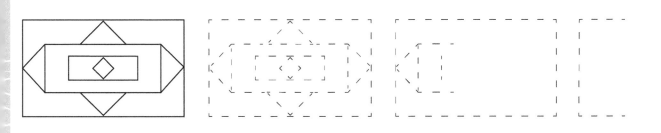

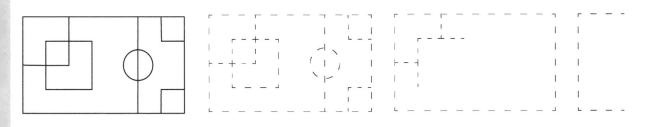

Complete the figure according to the model.

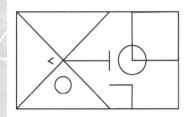  

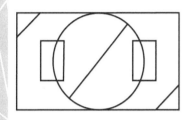 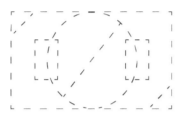 

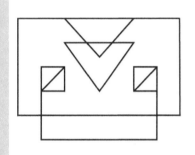  

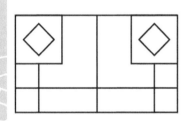 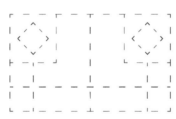 

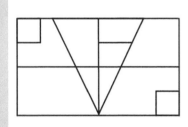 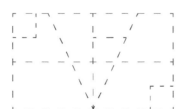 

Copy the strokes at the bottom guiding yourself from the model.

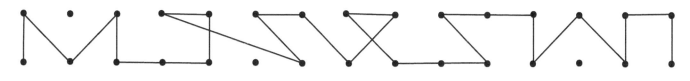

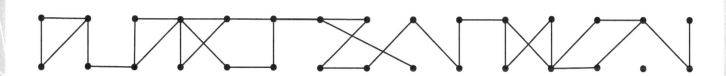

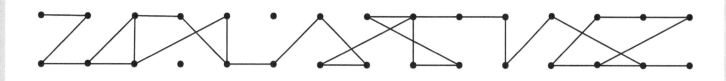

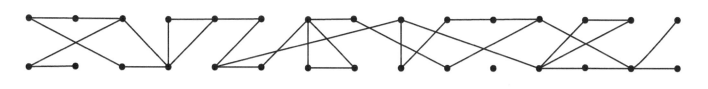

Copy the drawing on the left into the box on the right.

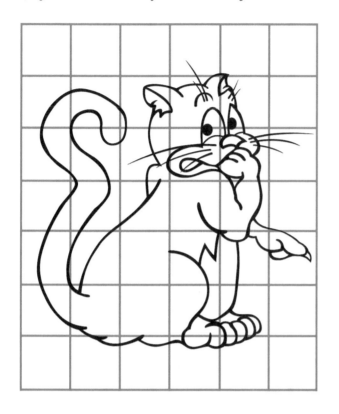

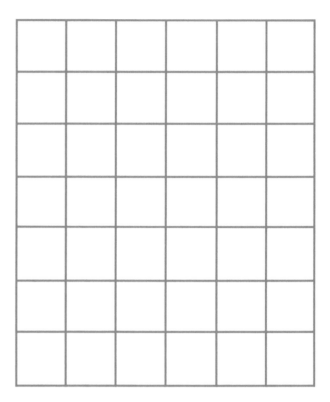

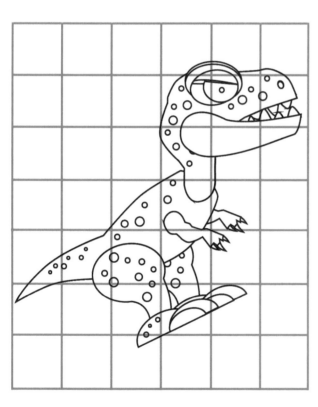

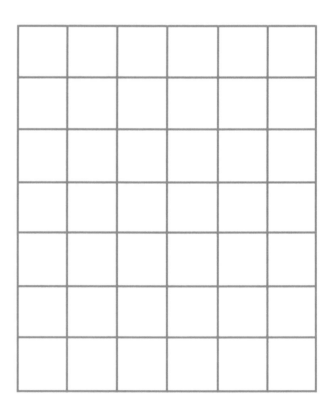

Completes the other half

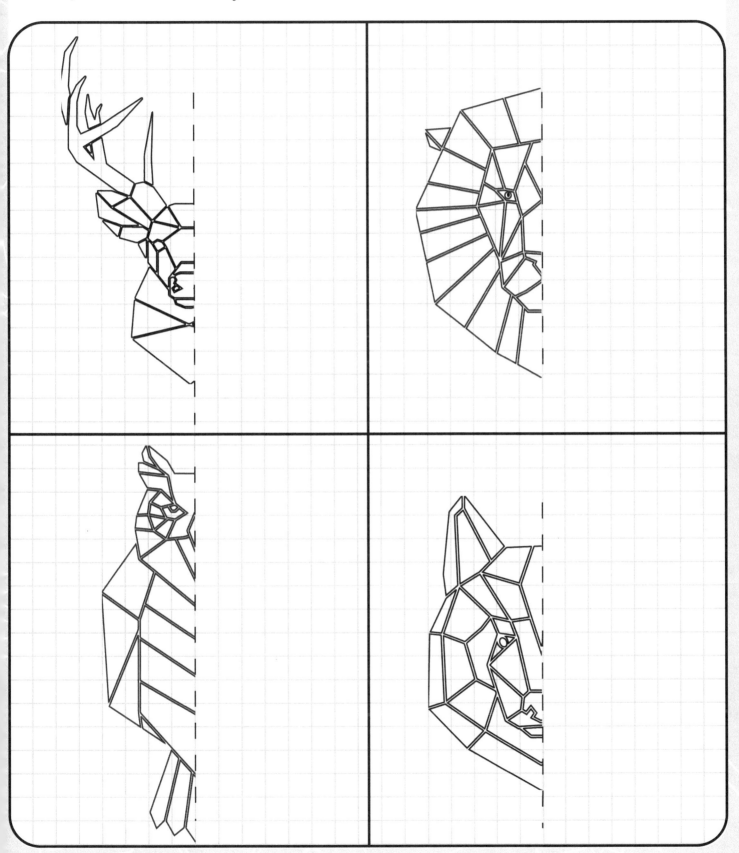

Trace the numbers following the example.

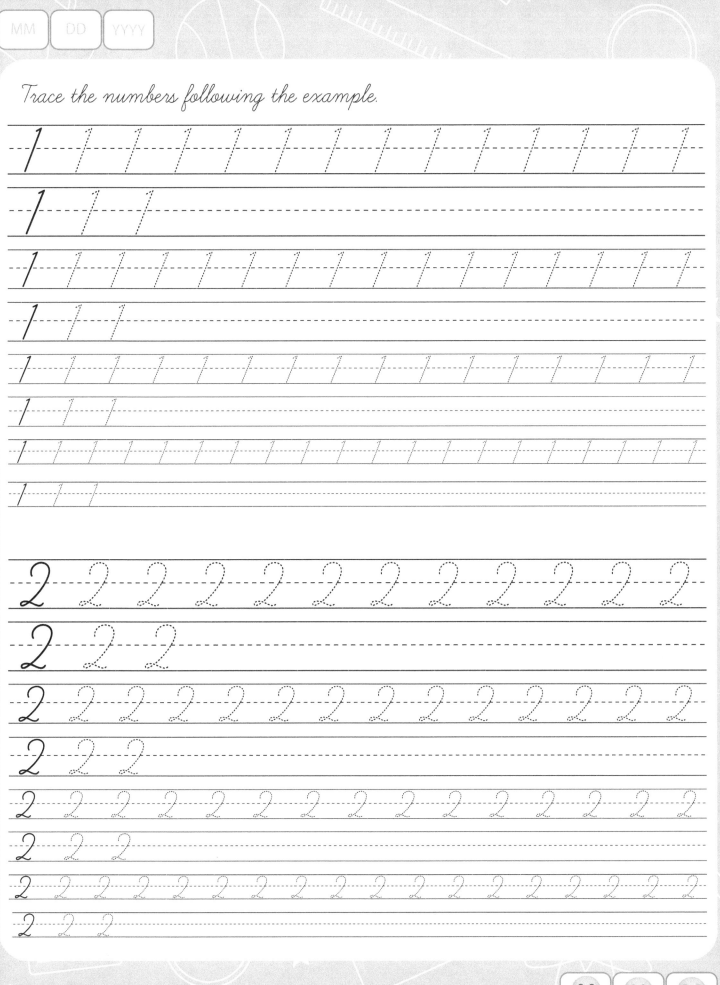

Trace the numbers following the example.

3 3 3 3 3 3 3 3 3 3 3 3 3

3 3 3

3 3 3 3 3 3 3 3 3 3 3 3 3

3 3 3

3 3 3 3 3 3 3 3 3 3 3 3 3

3 3 3

3 3 3 3 3 3 3 3 3 3 3 3 3

3 3 3

4 4 4 4 4 4 4 4 4 4 4 4 4

4 4 4

4 4 4 4 4 4 4 4 4 4 4 4 4

4 4 4

4 4 4 4 4 4 4 4 4 4 4 4 4

4 4 4

4 4 4 4 4 4 4 4 4 4 4 4 4

4 4 4

Trace the numbers following the example.

Trace the numbers following the example.

7 7 7 7 7 7 7 7 7 7 7 7 7 7

7 7 7

7 7 7 7 7 7 7 7 7 7 7 7 7 7

7 7 7

7 7 7 7 7 7 7 7 7 7 7 7 7 7

7 7 7

7 7 7 7 7 7 7 7 7 7 7 7 7 7

7 7 7

8 8 8 8 8 8 8 8 8 8 8 8 8 8

8 8 8

8 8 8 8 8 8 8 8 8 8 8 8 8 8

8 8 8

8 8 8 8 8 8 8 8 8 8 8 8 8 8

8 8 8

8 8 8 8 8 8 8 8 8 8 8 8 8 8

8 8 8

Trace the numbers following the example.

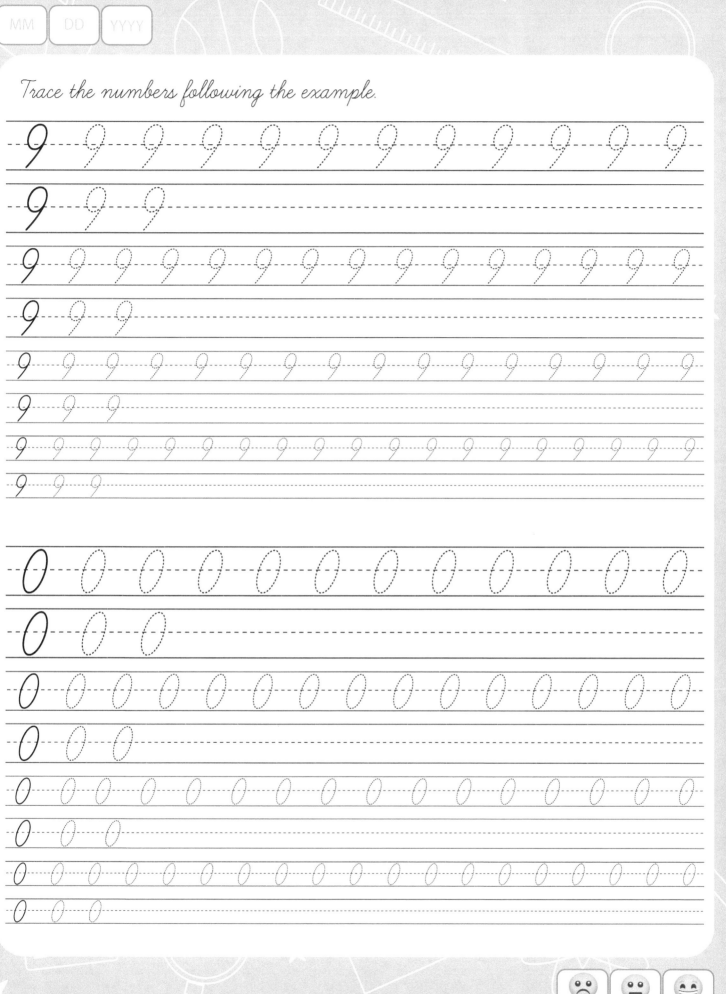

LEVEL 3

Alphabet

Here you will learn to:

 Write the alphabet in cursive using the dot to dot method, tracing and copying each letter in lowercase and uppercase.

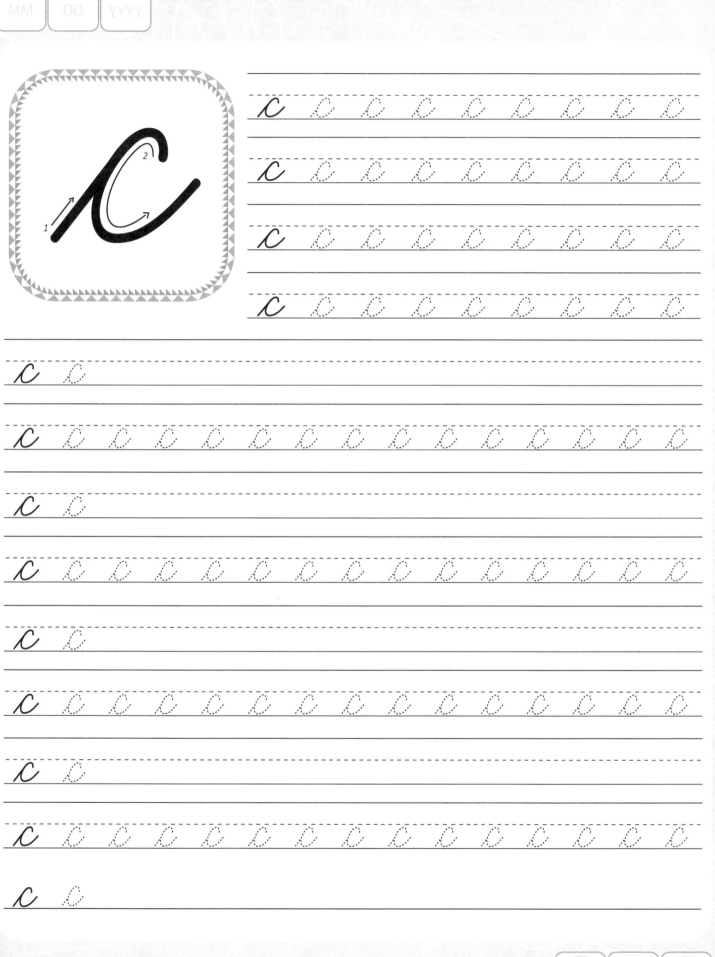

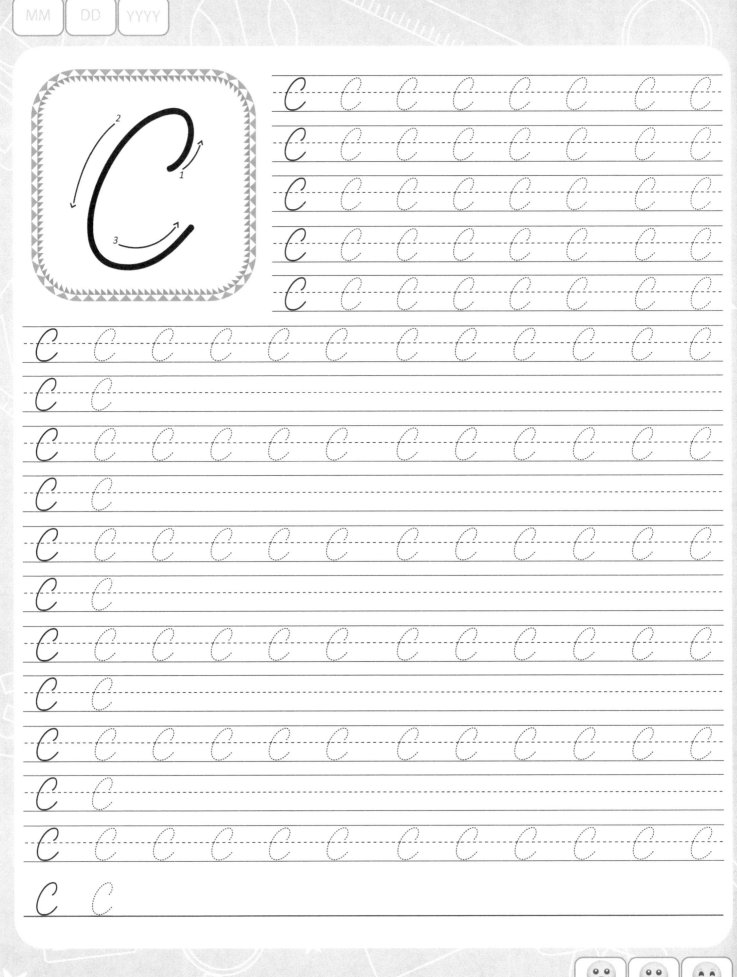

d

d d d d d d d d d
d d d d d d d d d
d d d d d d d d d
d d d d d d d d d

d d

d d d d d d d d d d d d d d

d d

d d d d d d d d d d d d d d

d d

d d d d d d d d d d d d d d

d d

d d d d d d d d d d d d d d

d d

h h h h h h h h
h h h h h h h h
h h h h h h h h
h h h h h h h h

h h
h h h h h h h h h h h h h
h h
h h h h h h h h h h h h h
h h
h h h h h h h h h h h h h
h h
h h h h h h h h h h h h h
h h

j

J

k k k k k k k k

k k k k k k k k

k k k k k k k k

k k k k k k k k

k k

k k k k k k k k k k k k k

k k

k k k k k k k k k k k k k

k k

k k k k k k k k k k k k k

k k

k k k k k k k k k k k k k

k k

ℓ

ℓ ℓ ℓ ℓ ℓ ℓ ℓ ℓ ℓ ℓ

ℓ ℓ ℓ ℓ ℓ ℓ ℓ ℓ ℓ ℓ

ℓ ℓ ℓ ℓ ℓ ℓ ℓ ℓ ℓ ℓ

ℓ ℓ ℓ ℓ ℓ ℓ ℓ ℓ ℓ ℓ

ℓ ℓ

ℓ ℓ ℓ ℓ ℓ ℓ ℓ ℓ ℓ ℓ ℓ ℓ ℓ ℓ

ℓ ℓ

ℓ ℓ ℓ ℓ ℓ ℓ ℓ ℓ ℓ ℓ ℓ ℓ ℓ ℓ

ℓ ℓ

ℓ ℓ ℓ ℓ ℓ ℓ ℓ ℓ ℓ ℓ ℓ ℓ ℓ ℓ

ℓ ℓ

ℓ ℓ ℓ ℓ ℓ ℓ ℓ ℓ ℓ ℓ ℓ ℓ ℓ ℓ

ℓ ℓ

m m m m m m m

m m m m m m m

m m m m m m m

m m m m m m m

m m

m m m m m m m m m m

m m

m m m m m m m m m

m m

m m m m m m m m m m

m m

m m m m m m m m m m

m m

n

n n n n n n n n

n n n n n n n n

n n n n n n n n

n n n n n n n n

n n

n n n n n n n n n n n n

n n

n n n n n n n n n n n n

n n

n n n n n n n n n n n n

n n

n n n n n n n n n n n n

n n

n n

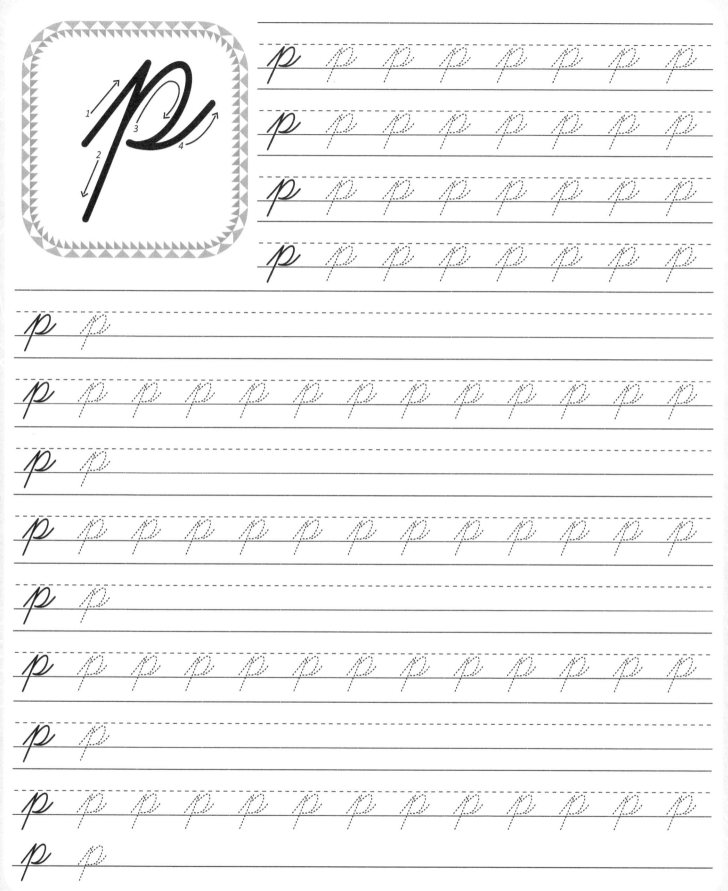

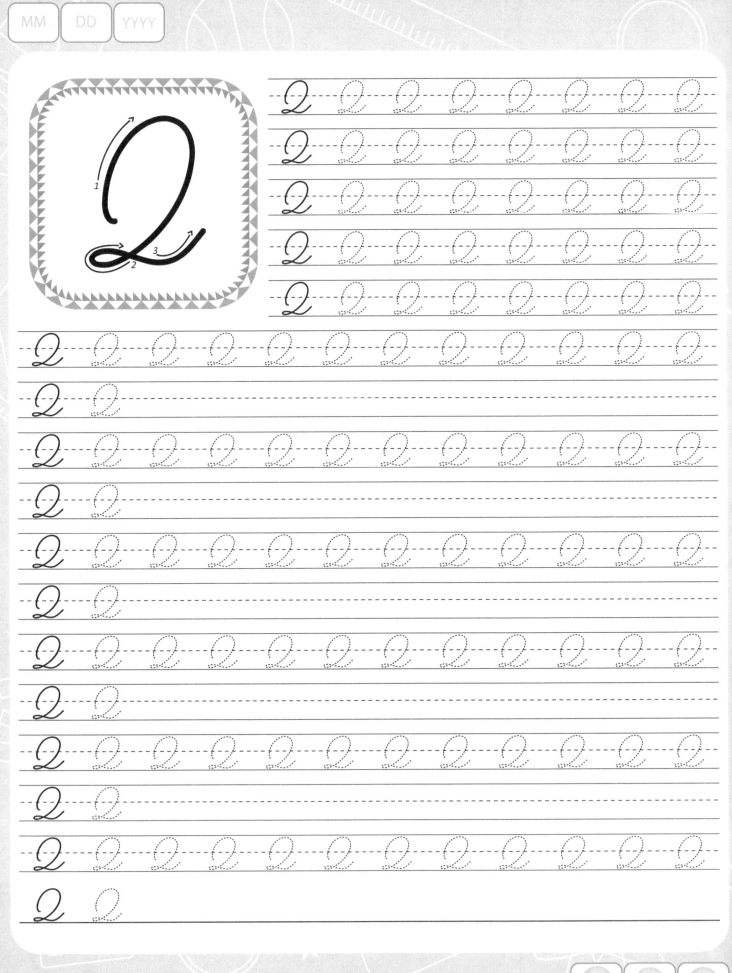

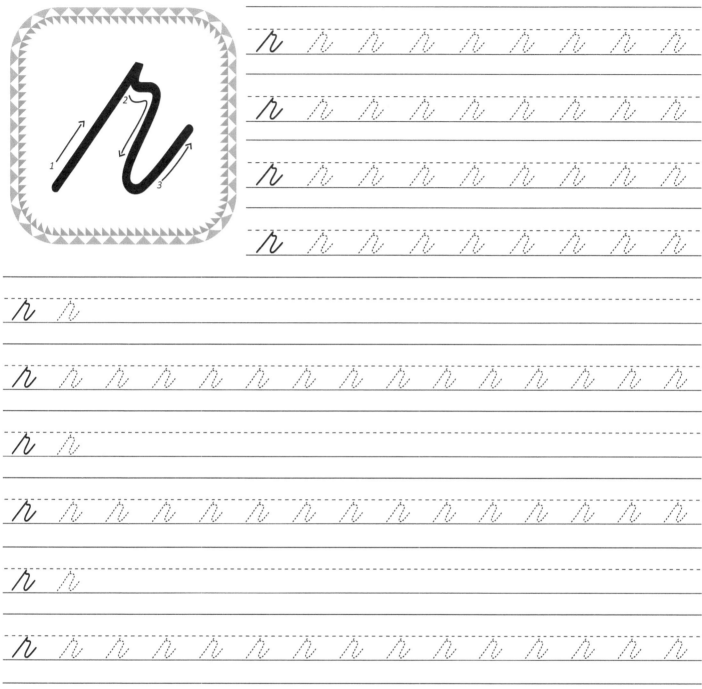

π

𝓉 𝓉 𝓉 𝓉 𝓉 𝓉 𝓉 𝓉 𝓉 𝓉

𝓉 𝓉 𝓉 𝓉 𝓉 𝓉 𝓉 𝓉 𝓉 𝓉

𝓉 𝓉 𝓉 𝓉 𝓉 𝓉 𝓉 𝓉 𝓉 𝓉

𝓉 𝓉 𝓉 𝓉 𝓉 𝓉 𝓉 𝓉 𝓉 𝓉

𝓉 𝓉

𝓉 𝓉 𝓉 𝓉 𝓉 𝓉 𝓉 𝓉 𝓉 𝓉 𝓉 𝓉 𝓉 𝓉 𝓉

𝓉 𝓉

𝓉 𝓉 𝓉 𝓉 𝓉 𝓉 𝓉 𝓉 𝓉 𝓉 𝓉 𝓉 𝓉 𝓉

𝓉 𝓉

𝓉 𝓉 𝓉 𝓉 𝓉 𝓉 𝓉 𝓉 𝓉 𝓉 𝓉 𝓉 𝓉 𝓉

𝓉 𝓉

𝓉 𝓉 𝓉 𝓉 𝓉 𝓉 𝓉 𝓉 𝓉 𝓉 𝓉 𝓉 𝓉 𝓉 𝓉

𝓉 𝓉

$\mathcal{M}$

$\mathcal{UU}$

Y Y Y Y Y Y Y

Y Y Y Y Y Y Y

Y Y Y Y Y Y Y

Y Y

Y Y Y Y Y Y Y Y Y Y

Y Y

Y Y Y Y Y Y Y Y Y Y

Y Y

Y Y Y Y Y Y Y Y Y Y

Y Y

Y Y Y Y Y Y Y Y Y Y

Y Y

LEVEL 4

Words

Here you will learn to:

 Write words in cursive with all the letters of the alphabet from A to Z

 Connect between two to nine letters per word

 Expand your vocabulary by knowing new word

Ab   Ab   Ab   Ab   Ab   Ab   Ab   Ab

Abrasive   Absolute   Abstract   Ability

Ac   Ac   Ac   Ac   Ac   Ac   Ac   Ac

Accessory   Acrobat   Accuse   Accumulate

Ad   Ad   Ad   Ad   Ad   Ad   Ad

Advantage   Adventure   Advance   Address

Ae   Ae   Ae   Ae   Ae   Ae   Ae

Aerobic   Aerospace   Aerosol   Aerial

Af   Af   Af   Af   Af   Af   Af

Affect   Afford   Afternoon   After

Ba Ba Ba Ba Ba Ba Ba Ba

Backstage   Baggage   Ballad   Battery

Be Be Be Be Be Be Be Be

Beaming   Beyond   Beloved   Benefit

Bi Bi Bi Bi Bi Bi Bi Bi

Biography   Bishop   Bitter   Bicycle

Bo Bo Bo Bo Bo Bo Bo Bo

Boxer   Boast   Boyfriend   Boundary

Bu Bu Bu Bu Bu Bu Bu Bu

Button   Business   Bulletin   Bustle

Ca Ca Ca Ca Ca Ca Ca Ca

Castle Cathedral Campaign Capture

Ce Ce Ce Ce Ce Ce Ce Ce

Celebrity Center Certain Ceiling

Ci Ci Ci Ci Ci Ci Ci Ci

Circus Citizen Circuit Civilize

Co Co Co Co Co Co Co Co

Condolence Coffe Conscience Cold

Cu Cu Cu Cu Cu Cu Cu Cu

Customer Cute Culture Cunning

Da Da Da Da Da Da Da Da

Danger   Dance   Darling   Damnify

De De De De De De De De

Deception   Deluxe   Defame   Debonair

Di Di Di Di Di Di Di Di

Dinosaur   Dinner   Dialect   Diligence

Do Do Do Do Do Do Do Do

Dodge   Doghouse   Document   Dormitory

Du Du Du Du Du Du Du Du

Dust   Dummy   Duplicity   Durability

Ea   Ea   Ea   Ea   Ea   Ea   Ea   Ea

Earth   Early   Easter   Easy   Eavesdrop

Eb   Eb   Eb   Eb   Eb   Eb   Eb   Eb

Ebullinese   Ebb   Ebony   Ebullient

Ec   Ec   Ec   Ec   Ec   Ec   Ec   Ec

Ecosystem   Ecstacy   Eclair   Ecclesiastical

Ed   Ed   Ed   Ed   Ed   Ed   Ed   Ed

Edify   Edifice   Edification   Educational

Ef   Ef   Ef   Ef   Ef   Ef   Ef   Ef

Effervescence   Effort   Efficiency   Effect

Fa   Fa   Fa   Fa   Fa   Fa   Fa   Fa

Famous   Fantastic   Farewell   Favorite

Fe   Fe   Fe   Fe   Fe   Fe   Fe   Fe

Felicity   Feast   Fence   Fecundate

Fi   Fi   Fi   Fi   Fi   Fi   Fi   Fi

Fiddle   Fiction   Fidelity   Fifteen

Fo   Fo   Fo   Fo   Fo   Fo   Fo   Fo

Forest   Forsake   Football   Foundation

Fu   Fu   Fu   Fu   Fu   Fu   Fu   Fu

Fullnes   Furniture   Fulfillment   Fullback

Ga Ga Ga Ga Ga Ga Ga Ga

Gardener Galaxy Garland Gastric

Ge Ge Ge Ge Ge Ge Ge Ge

Geometry Gender Genius Gestate

Gi Gi Gi Gi Gi Gi Gi Gi

Ginger Giant Gifted Girlfriend

Go Go Go Go Go Go Go Go

Goodness Gossip Godchild Governing

Gu Gu Gu Gu Gu Gu Gu Gu

Guess Gunman Guesthouse Guidance

Ha Ha Ha Ha Ha Ha Ha Ha

Habitant Hamburger Happy Harvest

He He He He He He He He

Heritage Heaven Herald Hesitate

Hi Hi Hi Hi Hi Hi Hi Hi

Hitch Hidden Hispanic History

Ho Ho Ho Ho Ho Ho Ho Ho

Holiday Hospital Homage Housing

Hu Hu Hu Hu Hu Hu Hu Hu

Huge Humming Hunger Hurry Hurt

Id Id Id Id Id Id Id Id

Ideology   Idealize   Idolatry   Idiom

Im Im Im Im Im Im Im Im

Image   Imitate   Impasse   Impact

In In In In In In In In

Infinite   Increase   Incite   Instant

Ir Ir Ir Ir Ir Ir Ir Ir

Irony   Irradiate   Irresolvable   Irritate

Is Is Is Is Is Is Is Is

Island   Isolate   Issue   Islander

Ja Ja Ja Ja Ja Ja Ja Ja

Jackal Jacket Japanese Jawbone

Je Je Je Je Je Je Je Je

Jealous Jeans Jelly Jerk Jewel

Ji Ji Ji Ji Ji Ji Ji Ji

Jigsaw Jingle Jigsaw Jingle

Jo Jo Jo Jo Jo Jo Jo Jo

Jockey Joinder Journal Joyless

Ju Ju Ju Ju Ju Ju Ju Ju

Juggler Justify Juvenile Jungle

Ka Ka Ka Ka Ka Ka Ka Ka

Kaki Kangaroo Karat Kayac

Ke Ke Ke Ke Ke Ke Ke Ke

Keen Key Keep Kermess Keen

Ki Ki Ki Ki Ki Ki Ki Ki

Kitchen Kindergarten Kiss Kidney

Ko Ko Ko Ko Ko Ko Ko Ko

Koala Korean Koran Koala

Kn Kn Kn Kn Kn Kn Kn Kn

Knack Kneecap Knighthood Knowing

La La La La La La La La

Launch Labyrinth Latitude Lather

Le Le Le Le Le Le Le Le

Legion Lead Leopard Leukemia

Li Li Li Li Li Li Li Li

License Lifesaver Like Litigant

Lo Lo Lo Lo Lo Lo Lo Lo

Logotype Lovable Logarithm Lotion

Lu Lu Lu Lu Lu Lu Lu Lu

Lucid Lucrative Luscious Luminous

Ma Ma Ma Ma Ma Ma Ma Ma

Mackinstosh Magic Majestic Marathon

Me Me Me Me Me Me Me Me

Meet Member Merchandise Metabolism

Mi Mi Mi Mi Mi Mi Mi Mi

Microscope Mildew Minimal Mishap

Mo Mo Mo Mo Mo Mo Mo Mo

Mobile Modulate Monotone Mountain

Mu Mu Mu Mu Mu Mu Mu Mu

Middler Mulberry Mummify Munition

Na   Na   Na   Na   Na   Na   Na   Na

Narrative   Nascent   Nativity   Navigable

Ne   Ne   Ne   Ne   Ne   Ne   Ne   Ne

Nestling   Negation   Neurology   Network

Ni   Ni   Ni   Ni   Ni   Ni   Ni   Ni

Nightingale   Nimble   Nickname   Nippers

No   No   No   No   No   No   No   No

Nogood   Notable   Notoriety   November

Nu   Nu   Nu   Nu   Nu   Nu   Nu   Nu

Number   Nuptial   Nurture   Nutrient

Oa Oa Oa Oa Oa Oa Oa Oa

Oasis Oatmeal Oak Oath Oar

Ob Ob Ob Ob Ob Ob Ob Ob

Obedience Oblivion Obstinacy Obvious

Oc Oc Oc Oc Oc Oc Oc Oc

Occident Occupation October Octopus

Od Od Od Od Od Od Od Od

Odds Odious Odyssey Odoriferous

Of Of Of Of Of Of Of Of

Office Offset Offspring Officiate

Pa Pa Pa Pa Pa Pa Pa Pa

Paradise Palace Panhandle Password

Pe Pe Pe Pe Pe Pe Pe Pe

Pedestal Pelican Perseverance Petulance

Pi Pi Pi Pi Pi Pi Pi Pi

Pincers Pigheaded Pincush Pioneer

Po Po Po Po Po Po Po Po

Poignant Poison Polyclinic Possibility

Pu Pu Pu Pu Pu Pu Pu Pu

Punish Puzzle Purvey Pumpkin

Qua Qua Qua Qua Qua Qua Qua Qua

Quarantine Quandary Quartz Qualitative

Que Que Que Que Que Que Que Que

Quest Queen Querulous Questionable

Qui Qui Qui Qui Qui Qui Qui Qui

Quick Quintet Quizzical Quitclaim

Quo Quo Quo Quo Quo Quo Quo Quo

Quota Quotable Quotidian Quotient

Qua Qua Qua Qua Qua Qua Qua Qua

Quarantine Quandary Quartz Qualitative

Ra Ra Ra Ra Ra Ra Ra Ra

Random Rapport Radiogram Ratification

Re Re Re Re Re Re Re Re

Ready Rebuff Recapitulate Reliabilit

Ri Ri Ri Ri Ri Ri Ri Ri

Ridicule Riddle Rigorous Ringleader

Ro Ro Ro Ro Ro Ro Ro Ro

Rocket Rosebush Rotten Roundup Rover

Ru Ru Ru Ru Ru Ru Ru Ru

Runner Runway Rugged Rupture Rustic

Sa Sa Sa Sa Sa Sa Sa Sa

Sabotage Savage Savings Sanctification

Se Se Se Se Se Se Se Se

Season Sensation Seamstress Secretary

Si Si Si Si Si Si Si Si

Simulate Sinister Sixteenth Sizable

So So So So So So So So

Soldier Solvency Somersault Souvenir

Su Su Su Su Su Su Su Su

Surprise Superficial Supremacy Survive

Ta Ta Ta Ta Ta Ta Ta Ta

Tangerine Tardiness Talent Taxpayer

Te Te Te Te Te Te Te Te

Temple Tenderness Tedious Terrestrial

Ti Ti Ti Ti Ti Ti Ti Ti

Timber Titanium Tighten Tiresome

To To To To To To To To

Tolerance Tomorrow Torrent Towboat

Tu Tu Tu Tu Tu Tu Tu Tu

Turbulence Tulip Turnover Tussle

Ul Ul Ul Ul Ul Ul Ul Ul

Ultimate   Ultraviolet   Ulcer   Ultraism

Un Un Un Un Un Un Un Un

Unbalance   Uncover   Universal   Untold

Up Up Up Up Up Up Up Up

Update   Upset   Upkeep   Uphold   Uprisal

Ur Ur Ur Ur Ur Ur Ur Ur

Urgency   Urology   Urban   Urge   Urine

Ut Ut Ut Ut Ut Ut Ut Ut

Utility   Utmost   Utter   Utterance   Utterly

Va Va Va Va Va Va Va Va

Vacation   Valley   Valiant   Varnishing

Ve Ve Ve Ve Ve Ve Ve Ve

Venture   Velocity   Vehicle   Vertebrate

Vi Vi Vi Vi Vi Vi Vi Vi

Viewless   Village   Visualize   Vitaminic

Vo Vo Vo Vo Vo Vo Vo Vo

Vogue   Voltage   Voluntary   Voucher

Vu Vu Vu Vu Vu Vu Vu Vu

Vulcanize   Vulgar   Vulnerability   Vulture

Wa Wa Wa Wa Wa Wa Wa Wa

Wager   Walkover   Warehouse   Waterfront

We We We We We We We We

Welcome   Werewolf   Wetness   Welfare

Wi Wi Wi Wi Wi Wi Wi Wi

Wilderness   Wisdom   Winner   Wizardry

Wo Wo Wo Wo Wo Wo Wo Wo

Worship   Womanhood   Wonder   Workroom

Wr Wr Wr Wr Wr Wr Wr Wr

Wrapping   Wreck   Written   Wrought

Xe Xe Xe Xe Xe Xe Xe Xe

Xerography Xenophilia Xenophobe Xenophobia

Xy Xy Xy Xy Xy Xy Xy Xy

Xylographic Xylophage Xylophone Xylene

Xe Xe Xe Xe Xe Xe Xe Xe

Xerography Xenophilia Xenophobe Xenophobia

Xy Xy Xy Xy Xy Xy Xy Xy

Xylographic Xylophage Xylophone Xylene

Xe Xe Xe Xe Xe Xe Xe Xe

Xerography Xenophilia Xenophobe Xenophobia

Ya Ya Ya Ya Ya Ya Ya Ya
Yardage Yardstik Yachting Yahoo

Ye Ye Ye Ye Ye Ye Ye Ye
Yellow Yesterday Yearbook Yearning

Yi Yi Yi Yi Yi Yi Yi Yi
Yiel Yielding Yiel Yielding

Yo Yo Yo Yo Yo Yo Yo Yo
Yokefellow Young Youthful Youl

Ya Ya Ya Ya Ya Ya Ya Ya
Yardage Yardstik Yachting Yahoo

Za Za Za Za Za Za Za Za

Zany Zap Zany Zap Zany

Ze Ze Ze Ze Ze Ze Ze Ze

Zebra Zenith Zestful Zero Zest

Zi Zi Zi Zi Zi Zi Zi Zi

Zigzag Zing Zipper Zippy Zinc

Zo Zo Zo Zo Zo Zo Zo Zo

Zodiac Zombie Zoology Zoom Zoo

Za Za Za Za Za Za Za Za

Zany Zap Zany Zap Zany

LEVEL 5

Sentences

Here you will learn to:

 Practice cursive writing by copying inspirational quotes from famous people that will make you think and reflect on life.

"There is only one hapiness in this life, to love and to be loved" — George Sand —

There is only one hapiness in this life, to love and to be loved

"Always make a total effort. Even when the odds are against you" — Arnold Palmer —

Always make a total effort. Even when the odds are against you

"*Every child is an artist. The problem is how to remain an artist once he grows up*" – Pablo Picasso –

Every child is an artist. The problem is how to remain an artist once he grows up

"*With love and patience, nothing is impossible*"
– Daisaku Ikeda –

With love and patience, nothing is impossible

"To live a creative life, we must lose our fear of being wrong" — Joseph Chilton —

To live a creative life, we must lose our fear of being wrong

"There are no shortcuts to any place worth going" — Beverly Sills —

There are no shortcuts to any place worth going

"You are never too old to set another goal or to dream a new dream" — C. S. Lewis —

You are never too old to set another goal or to

dream a new dream

"Never let your memories be bigger than your dreams" — Douglas Ivester —

Never let your memories be bigger than your dreams

"Everyone sees what you appear, but few see what you really are"
– Niccolo Machiavelli –

Everyone sees what you appear, but few see what you really are

"Creativity is intelligence having fun"
– Albert Einstein –

Creativity is intelligence having fun

"Travel makes one modest. You see what a tiny place you occupy in the world" — Gustav Flaubert —

Travel makes one modest. You see what a tiny place you occupy in the world

"Take only memories, leave only footprints"
— Chief Seattle —

Take only memories, leave only footprints

"Always turn a negative situation into a positive situation" – Michael Jordan –

Always turn a negative situation into a positive situation

"Jobs fill your pocket, but adventures fill your soul"
Jamie Lyn Beatty

Jobs fill your pocket, but adventures fill your soul

"The measure of who we are is what we do with what we have" — Vince Lombardi —

The measure of who we are is what we do with what we have

"Once you choose hope, anything's posible" — Christopher Reeve —

Once you choose hope, anything's posible

"Learn how to be happy with what you have while you pursue all that you want" – Jim Rohn –

Learn how to be happy with what you have while you pursue all that you want

"Turn your wounds into wisdom"
– Oprah Winfrey –

Turn your wounds into wisdom

"Start wide, expand further, and never look back"
– Arnold Schwarzenegger –

Start wide, expand further, and never look back

"Eighty percent of success is showing up"
– Woody Allen –

Eighty percent of success is showing up

"The best way to predict the future is to invent it"

– Alan Kay –

The best way to predict the future is to invent it

"A goal is a dream with a deadline"

– Napoleon Hill –

A goal is a dream with a deadline

"*Innovation distinguishes between a leader and a follower*"
— Steve Jobs —

Innovation distinguishes between a leader and a follower

"*Don't dream your life, but live your dream*"
— Mark Twain —

Don't dream your life, but live your dream

"Trust in dreams, for in them is hidden the gate to eternity"

– Khalil Gibran –

Trust in dreams, for in them is hidden the gate to
eternity

"Who seeks shall find"

– Sófocles –

Who seeks shall find

"Don't let yesterday take up too much of today"

– Will Rogers –

Don't let yesterday take up too much of today

"The power of imagination makes us infinite"

– John Muir –

The power of imagination makes us infinite

"*Everything seems impossible until it is done*"

– Nelson Mandela –

Everything seems impossible until it is done

"*Change your thoughts and you change your world*"

– Norman Vincent Peale –

Change your thoughts and you change your world

"Blessed are the curious for they shall have adventures"

– Lovelle Drachman –

Blessed are the curious for they shall have adventures

"If you have no critics you'll likely have no success"

– Malcolm X –

If you have no critics you'll likely have no success

"Always seek out the seed of triumph in every adversity"

– Og Mandino –

Always seek out the seed of triumph in every

adversity

"Success is where preparation and opportunity meet"

– Bobby Unser –

Success is where preparation and opportunity meet

"*You just can't beat the person who never gives up*"

– Babe Ruth –

You just can't beat the person who never gives up

"*Aim for the moon. If you miss, you may hit a star*"

– W. Clement Stone –

Aim for the moon. If you miss, you may hit a star

"If there is no struggle, there is no progress"

– Frederick Douglass –

If there is no struggle, there is no progress

"Sometimes the heart sees what is invisible to the eye"
– Jackson Brown, Jr. –

Sometimes the heart sees what is invisible to the eye

"It is during our darkest moments that we must focus to see the light" – Aristotle –

It is during our darkest moments that we must focus to see the light

"Love is the beauty of the soul"
– San Agustin –

Love is the beauty of the soul

"Enthusiasm moves the world"
– Arthur Balfour –

Enthusiasm moves the world

SCORE TABLE

Level 1   ➡️   N° 😁 = ☐

Level 2   ➡️   N° 😁 = ☐

Level 3   ➡️   N° 😁 = ☐

Level 4   ➡️   N° 😁 = ☐

Level 5   ➡️   N° 😁 = ☐ **+**

TOTAL ☐

AWARDS

N°	MEDAL	AWARDS
_ _ _ _ _ _	*Gold*	
_ _ _ _ _ _	*Silver*	
_ _ _ _ _ _	*Bronze*	

Made in United States
Troutdale, OR
07/05/2024

21039989R00073